INDIA

UNPACKED

Susie Brooks

First published in 2013 by Wayland
Copyright © Wayland 2013

Wayland
338 Euston Road
London NW1 3BH

Wayland Australia
Level 17/207 Kent Street
Sydney, NSW 2000

Editors: Annabel Stones and Elizabeth Brent
Designer: Peter Clayman
Cover design by Matthew Kelly

Dewey categorisation: 954'.0532-dc23

ISBN 978 0 7502 7725 9

Printed in China

10 9 8 7 6 5 4 3 2 1

Picture acknowledgements: All images, including cover images and graphic elements, courtesy of Shutterstock except: p10 © AFP/Getty Images; p11 © Christopher Pillitz/In Pictures/Corbis (r); p19 © paulprescott72 (r); p22 © Getty Images (b); p26 © Arko Datta/Reuters/Corbis, © Isabelle Vayron/Sygma/Corbis (t); p28 © Indian School/Getty Images; p29 © Pramod R. Mistry/Getty Images (l)

The website addresses (URLs) included in this book were valid at the time of going to press. However, it is possible that contents or addresses may change following the publication of this book. No responsibility for any such changes can be accepted by either the author or the Publisher.

Wayland is a division of Hachette Children's Books, an Hachette UK company.
www.hachette.co.uk

Contents

India: Unpacked

Welcome to India - on a map it looks like a big triangle, poking out at the bottom of Asia! In real life it's a magical land of sense-smacking spices, mighty mountains, breathtaking buildings and roof-rattling rains. Wherever you go in India you'll find colour, curries, crafts… and cricket fans! So get ready to track down a tiger, race a rickshaw and check out some blockbusting Bollywood dance moves on the way!

Fact File

Flag:

Area: 3,287,263km²
Population: 1,220,800,359 (July 2013)
Capital city: New Delhi
Land Borders: 14,103km with six countries
Currency: The Rupee

India

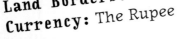

Useful Phrases

India has 22 official languages, but no single one is used everywhere! These phrases are in Hindi, the most widely spoken language.

Namaste - Hello/Goodbye
Aap kaise hain? - How are you?
Main theek hoon, dhanyavad - I'm fine, thank you
Kripaya - Please
Mira naam... ha - My name is...
Kya aap English bolte hain? - Do you speak English?
Fir milenge - See you later
Waah! - Great!

Try repeating this Hindi tongue twister!

"kaccha papad, pakka papad, kaccha papad, pakka papad..."

Cooked poppadom, uncooked poppadom, cooked poppadom, uncooked poppadom...

India is the birthplace of chess, snakes and ladders, yoga... and laughter yoga, where people get together and giggle!

Don't be charmed by a king cobra — the poison in its bite is enough to kill 20 people!

From 0 to a Billion

India is a place of colour, contrasts and crowds! More people live here than anywhere else except China, which it's likely to overtake soon. No one knows exactly when India was first inhabited, but we do know it was home to one of the oldest civilisations in the world. Now there are more than a billion people living in India. That's about one in every seven people on Earth!

NO WAY!

Many words in the English language came from India – pyjamas, dungarees, shampoo, bungalow and bangle are just a few!

Crowds fill a street in Delhi, India's capital city.

Ancient Indus

In 1856, railway workers in the Indus Valley dug up some old bricks. It turned out they belonged to a 5,000-year-old town! The people who once lived in this part of ancient India built many huge cities, complete with fortresses, wells and household loos. They developed their own language, farmed, traded and worshipped gods similar to the Hindu ones today. Unsurprisingly, 'Indus' is where India got its name.

You can see ruins from ancient Indus Valley cities in the area that's now Pakistan.

Colourful Past

Over the centuries, India has seen many changes in power. The Muslim Mughals, who ruled in the 1500s and 1600s, left behind great monuments such as the Taj Mahal. In the 1700s, a trading firm called the British East India Company gained control of the country. They made English the official language, and later India became part of the British Empire. The Indian railways and passion for cricket both began at this time!

It took 20,000 workers and 1,000 elephants to build the Taj Mahal!

Going it Alone

Pakistan was once a part of India. It was separated when the country became independent from Britain in 1947. Muslims were to live in Pakistan and Hindus in India – but there was conflict as many people lost their homes and land. About a million people died in the fighting or from gruelling journeys across the border. There are still tensions between India and Pakistan today.

7

Touring India

Picture a billion people all trying to get from A to B. OK, not everyone in India travels at once - but sometimes it can feel that way! Bus and train stations are noisy, hectic places where crowds tussle for tickets and seats. If a vehicle is full they'll still cram in more passengers - even if some have to cling to the outside! Savvy travellers book ahead, arrive early and don't always expect a smooth ride...

NO WAY!

India's rail routes cover about 64,000km - that would take you more than one-and-a-half times around the circumference of the Earth!

Reckless Rickshaws

'Sit tight!' is good advice for anyone riding in an autorickshaw. These nippy motorised 'tuk-tuks' dodge boldly in and out of city traffic. Drivers overtake buses, cars – and cows – with just millimetres to spare, and tend to use their horn before their brakes. Some intrepid tourists get tooting themselves in organised rickshaw races... it's one way to see the country, if you're brave!

Autorickshaws offer a colourful three-wheeled taxi service!

Right on Track

More than 25 million passengers hop aboard India's trains each day. They cram into carriages of all classes, from Unreserved (race for a seat!) to First Class AC, with carpeted cabins and beds. Whether you're chugging on a Himalayan steam train or racing on a high-speed express, every trip is an adventure. You won't go hungry, with tea and snack sellers wandering the aisles too!

You can enjoy scenery like this from a train in Goa.

Going Local

Indians are creative when it comes to local transport. It's normal to see a whole family on a motorbike, or people cycling with impossible-looking loads. In the northern hills, you can squeeze into a bone-rattling share-jeep; or take a riceboat along the sleepy waters of Kerala in the south. Ride a mule, a camel, or an elephant. Or, like many Indians, just make use of your feet!

In a share-jeep you pay for your seat – or roof space!

Everyone's Game

The traffic in India may be noisy, but wait till you hear a cricket crowd! Nothing matches the roar of excitement when India are batting well, never mind hockey (the national sport) or polo (invented here), although they are popular too. Indians live and breathe cricket. Whether they're watching it, playing it or just plain raving about it, it's a game that gets pulses racing countrywide!

The Men in Blue

The British brought cricket to India in the 1700s, and in 1932 the Indian team played (and lost) their first Test Match. Today India are ranked third in the world in Tests and first in One Day Internationals. The Men in Blue (yes, they wear blue shirts!), are worshipped in India. Even their rivals admit they're pretty good, with players like Sachin Tendulkar and Sunil Gavaskar rated among history's best.

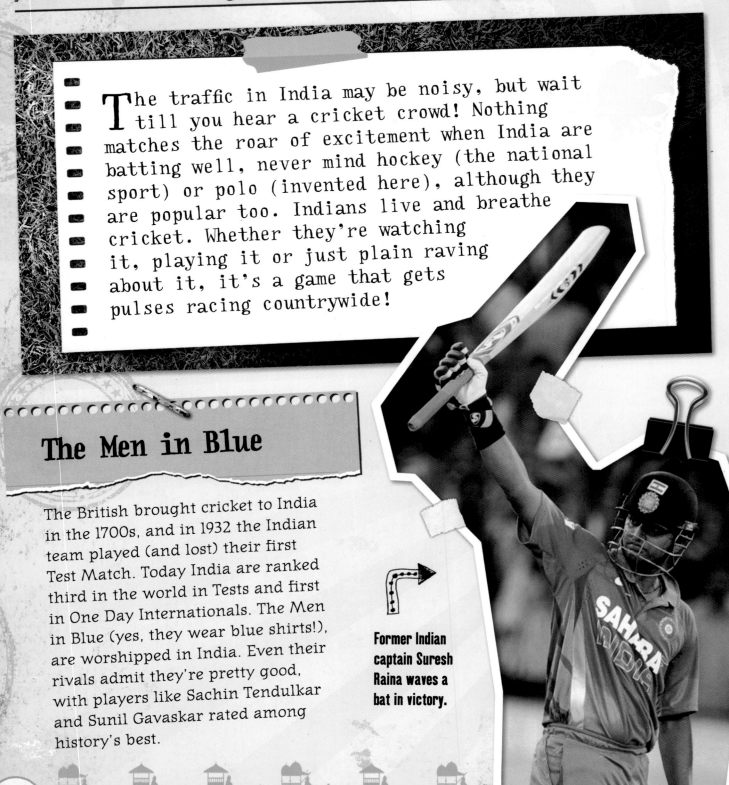

Former Indian captain Suresh Raina waves a bat in victory.

NO WAY!

At 2,444m above sea level, the cricket ground at Chail in northern India is the highest in the world. There's a polo pitch there too, if you like heights!

Twenty20

Twenty20 cricket is a whole different ball game. The shorter matches, played in just 20 overs, are showcased by the Indian Premier League. It's India's favourite tournament and the richest in cricket, paying top international players whopping fees to compete. Fans around the world watch the IPL on TV, and in 2010 it became the first sports event to be broadcast live on YouTube.

Teams stand to attention as their national anthem plays.

If you're going to be a cricket star, you have to practise hard!

Galli Games

Dried-up river beds, back alleys, beaches... it's hard to find a strip of land in India that hasn't been used for cricket! Children even play on roads, waiting for traffic to clear before slogging the ball. Street, or *galli*, cricket has no official rulebook. Stumps might be made from bins, bricks or bottles and a simple stick can be a bat.

Wild Wonders

With so many people in India, you might wonder how animals and plants fit in! In fact, much of the forest that once covered India has been cleared to make way for farmland, cities and roads. Many native species are now endangered, but look carefully and you'll still find some surprises.

Indian elephants are treasured beasts – some live in temples full-time! They eat a lot (about 150kg a day) and have excellent memories for journeys.

If you're a peafowl, it's best to be male – you get all the brightest feathers! The colourful peacock is India's national bird.

Beware the sharp teeth of the gharial – a thin-snouted type of croc. Males of this species have a bulge over their nostrils that makes a bizarre buzzing sound.

India's national flower is the lotus – often mistaken for a water lily. It's a symbol of wealth and fertility, sacred to Hindus, and a popular design for tattoos!

Mangroves are trees and shrubs that grow in swampy forests around India's coasts. Their tangled roots make them look as if they're standing on stilts above the water.

You can hear the roar of a Bengal tiger 3km away! Tigers hunt at night and can see six times better than us in the dark. Whether you can see them, with their camouflaged stripes, is another matter.

Rocks, Rivers and Rains

If you stretched out the coastline of India and its islands, it would reach further than from London to Delhi! That means a lot of beaches, and a fair few swamps and cliffs too. You'll also find mountains, deserts, rainforests... in fact most kinds of landscape you can imagine. It's amazing to think that the country was formed 50 million years ago when a drifting chunk of land collided with Asia!

In the high Himalayas, there's snow all year round.

Himalayan Heights

Up in the Himalayas (meaning 'home of snow'), you literally have your head in the clouds. India's highest peak is Kanchenjunga, at 8,586m. Expert climbers can scale it – but they stop just short of the summit, which is sacred to local people. The rest of us might try mountain biking, trekking or white-water rafting in the lower valleys. Or just enjoy the view across this 2,400km-long mountain range!

Wet Winds

Flooded streets are a fact of life during the monsoon season.

If you head to India between June and September, remember to take a raincoat! This is monsoon season, when winds sweep wet weather up the country and turn the landscape from brown to green. Downpours can last for days at first, then chop and change with steamy hours of sunshine. It's refreshing to get caught in a monsoon shower, but floods can be destructive at this time of year.

Ganga Ma

More than 400 million Indians rely on the Ganges River in some way. They depend on it for farming and industry, and as a holy place where pilgrims bathe and pray. Known as Ganga Ma (Mother Ganges), the river attracts thousands of worshippers each day. Unfortunately about a billion litres of raw sewage are deposited daily in the water too.

NO WAY!

The Himalayas are growing! Movements within the Earth push the mountains upwards by a few centimetres each year.

Pilgrims flock to the city of Varanasi, on the banks of the sacred Ganges.

Life on the Land

Ask people in India where they're from, and they'll often name their family village - even if they live in the city! Seven out of ten Indians live in rural areas, and they're very loyal to their roots. Farmers make up half of India's workforce, with many cultivating the fertile Ganges Plain. Crops grow well here, but it's still a struggle to feed everyone and many country people are very poor.

Popular Crops

Indians grow a lot of things, but their greatest grain is rice. You'll see families wading in bright green paddy fields, hand-sowing, reaping or spreading cow dung to fertilise the soil. India grows many different types of rice and is the second-largest producer after China. Another crop that's big here is tea. Head to hilly Darjeeling for the 'champagne' of teas, or to Assam if you like it strong!

It's usually women who pick the tea.

16

Some village houses are built on stilts to escape flooding.

Wandering Thar

Riding a camel is fun for tourists — and part of life for nomads in the Thar Desert. In fact, they use camels for milk, meat and wool too. These wandering people live where they find water. They herd sheep, goats and cattle and grow fruits, maize and other crops where they can. Visit during a desert festival and you'll find them singing, snake charming and competing for the best-dressed camel prize!

Camels are like removal vans for the Thar nomads!

Village Living

Where do 830 million people live in the Indian countryside? In at least 641,000 different villages! These farming communities have roles for everyone, from carpenters and barbers to priests and sweepers too. Typical houses are small, built of mud or wood, and often without electricity. There's a local well for water, and toilets tend to be shared. It helps to get on with the neighbours here!

High Tech, Low Tech!

India is experiencing boom times - not surprising, with a billion brains in the country! Many cities are now hotbeds of techno wizardry, while elsewhere people use some of the oldest working methods around...

Computers, TVs, washing machines... Indian factories make them all. They also produce the world's cheapest car – the Tata Nano.

Bangalore is India's Silicon Valley, with more than 200 software companies and a wealth of IT whizz-kids graduating from its colleges.

Indians from all walks of life love technology. You can catch even the poorest street seller chatting on a mobile phone – there are more than 860 million mobile users in the country!

If you struggle to balance a beanbag on your head, imagine carrying a pile of bricks! Women in India's construction industry do this all the time.

It can take 15 days to hand-spin a kilo of cotton. Nowadays there are quicker ways, but you'll still see people twirling spindles to turn lumps of fluff into yarn.

To plough a hectare of land in the traditional way, a farmer and his ox or water buffalo have to walk about 80km!

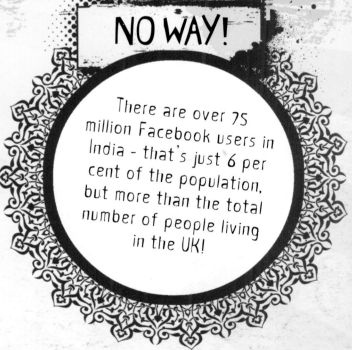

NO WAY!

There are over 75 million Facebook users in India – that's just 6 per cent of the population, but more than the total number of people living in the UK!

Staggering Cities

With their bustling streets, roaring traffic, roadside cooking and steamy heat, India's cities can send all your senses into overdrive! Home to less than a third of the population, there are still more than 50 cities of over a million people. Contrasts within them are plain to see - you'll find sparkling malls and mega-rich banks alongside beggars and slums.

The Red Fort was built as a palace for Mughal emperors in the 1600s.

Delhi Delights

More than 20 million people live in India's sprawling capital. Destroyed and rebuilt several times over the years, it's a medley of ancient and modern sights. In Old Delhi you can admire the great Mughal Red Fort or browse India's biggest spice market. New Delhi boasts splendid government buildings from the British era and... among other things... the International Toilet Museum!

Slum Life

Right in the centre of Mumbai sits Dharavi, a slum of a million people. About 293,000 of them, and who knows how many rats, cram into each square kilometre. It's surprisingly quiet as the streets are too narrow for traffic. Living conditions are dismal, but the residents are enterprising. You'll find them recycling, making soap, tanning leather, firing pots, taking tours... and that's just the start.

Dharavi's thriving industries mean that at least nine in ten people have a job!

NO WAY!

Dharavi's combined industries are worth an estimated billion US dollars! Junk comes to the slum's recycling plants from all around the world.

Hi Mumbai!

Built on what used to be seven islands, Mumbai was given to the British king, Charles II, on his marriage to a Portuguese princess in 1661. Now it's India's financial capital and a dynamic business city, where commuter trains carry 2.2 billion passengers a year. Attractions here include Bollywood film studios, the Gateway of India arch and a gigantic open-air laundry.

Mumbai is India's second-largest city.

Everyday India

You'll be pleased to know that children are highly valued in India! Sons are particularly good news, because they'll continue the family line. Life is based on sharing, with grandparents, cousins, uncles and aunts often living together under one roof. It's important to respect your elders and do your bit around the house. Traditionally, men are the breadwinners, though times are changing now.

More girls go to school now than they used to.

School or Skip

Imagine having one teacher to 60 pupils! That happens in many Indian schools. Primary education is free and compulsory, but millions of children still stay away and go to work. Help is at hand in some slums, where roving teachers take lessons in converted buses. At the other end of the scale, students at expensive boarding schools learn in luxury with WiFi and laptops in their rooms!

Match and Marry

Your parents have decided it's time for you to marry, so they've found you a bride or groom. Arranged marriages like this still happen in India, though couples usually get a say if they don't get on! Hindu people belong to groups called castes, and traditionally they must marry within them. If families can't find a suitable pairing, they might employ a professional matchmaker to help out.

Hindu wedding ceremonies often take place over several days.

NO WAY!

At the Hindu Karni Mata temple, 20,000 rats are fed daily with milk and sweets. The rats are believed to be holy - and it's lucky if one runs over your feet!

Fun with Faith

If the idea of a colossal paint fight sounds like fun to you, visit India during Holi! This is one of several Hindu festivals that turn the country into one big party. Two out of five Indians are Hindus, but the world's biggest Muslim population lives here too. You'll also meet Christians, Buddhists, Sikhs and Jains – plus a small number of Zoroastrians, who worship facing the Sun or a sacred fire.

People throw coloured powder and water at Holi!

Spice is Nice

If you're invited for a meal in an Indian home, here are a few things to remember: many Hindus are vegetarian, and no Hindus eat beef. Muslims don't eat pork. Never eat with your left hand - it's unhygienic. Feel free to use your fingers (many say food tastes better that way) and in some places burping is polite too! Expect to help yourself from a tableful of dishes - and when you really can't eat any more, please try to!

NO WAY!

Animal-loving Jains are all vegetarians - some monks even cover their mouths with a piece of cloth so they don't accidentally swallow an insect.

Sauce 'n' Spice

The British made up the word 'curry'. It comes from the South Indian *kari*, meaning 'sauce' – but we're not talking basic ketchup. Cumin, coriander, ginger, garlic, cardamom, fenugreek... the spice list goes on! Add tomatoes, onions, whatever meat or veg you like and as much chilli as you can take. But remember, Indian food is more about regional flavours than making your eyes and nose stream!

In South India, your food might be served on a banana leaf!

Sweet Treats

Got a sweet tooth?
Welcome to paradise! These
are just a few things to try:

Barfi – cubes of condensed milk
cooked with cardamom, fruit or nuts
and sometimes wrapped in edible foil.

Laddu – sugar, flour and coconut,
cooked in *ghee* (clear butter) and
rolled into colourful balls.

Kulfi – milky ice cream,
traditionally frozen in small metal
cans and sold by *kulfiwalas*.

Lassi – a yoghurt-based drink
that can be sweet or savoury.
Mango is a popular flavour!

In Indian markets you
buy spices by the scoop.

Each tiffin box is coded so it gets
to the right hungry person!

Lunch Bunch

Workers in India look forward to their tiffin
box at lunchtime. Inside this neat stack of
tins they might find home-cooked lentil
daal, curry, breads, rice, yoghurt, chutney
and often a sweet or two. In Mumbai, 5,000
dabbawalas ('tiffin workers') deliver more
than 350,000 lunch boxes a day. Each
box travels from the client's home to the
office and back via a relay of *dabbawallas*
rushing around on foot, bikes and trains!

Bollywood Beats

Where is the world's movie capital? No, not Hollywood - Bollywood! India's celebrated film industry churns out twice as many productions each year as its American counterpart. Indians love the cinema, buying around 7.5 million tickets per day. Their home-grown movies are glitzy, glamorous and dramatic displays of traditional music and dance with a modern twist!

NO WAY!

You don't have to be Indian to feature in a Bollywood film. Scouts in Mumbai are always looking for foreigners to be extras. Better get practising those dance moves!

Musical Melodramas

Star-crossed lovers, heroes and villains, fighting families and dreams coming true – you'll often spot these in a Bollywood plot! Spice them up with some catchy song-and-dance numbers and you've got a 3 or 4-hour movie that can attract 3 billion viewers worldwide. Casts are massive, but it's the big-name actors who steal the show and the mega-bucks. Stars like Shah Rukh Kahn rake in US$5 million per film!

Most Bollywood movies are filmed in the Hindi language.

Classic Sounds

Bollywood songs are up there with Hindi pop (or Indi-pop) for getting Indians on their feet. Their modern sounds still draw from Indian classical music, which is made up of three parts. The melody is played by strings like the sitar or a bamboo bansuri flute, while tabla drums beat out the rhythm. The tanpura (like a sitar but with fewer strings) holds a long drone note throughout the tune.

Musicians play the sitar and tabla drums in a classical Indian band.

Dance Secrets

Everything ripples and shimmies in Indian dance. It's like a fast-paced flow of snaking arms, swaying hips and graceful neck moves. To get the gist, look for the different shapes that dancers make with their hands. They create a kind of sign language, with facial expressions helping to tell the story. Feet have to learn a series of flexes, hops and kicks, with some steps bobbing along chicken-style!

Bells on the dancer's ankles jingle as she moves.

Bright Arts

Getting dressed in India can be an art form in itself! From rich embroidered silks to golden jewels, Indians make what they wear into something beautiful. The same goes for crafts, paintings, statues and buildings too. An Indian carver can turn a rock into an elephant... inside an elephant... inside an elephant! Detail is everything, and it's hard to find a more colourful country in the world.

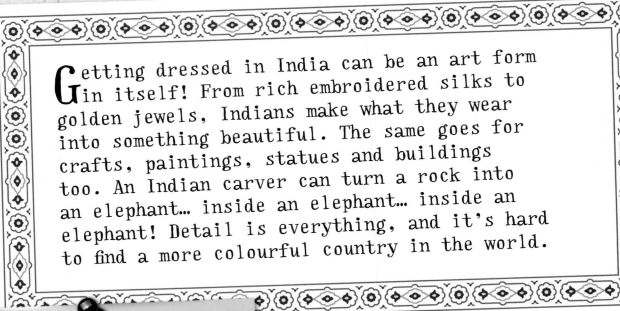

Magical Miniatures

Things don't get much more fiddly than an Indian miniature painting. Even on a picture as small as a credit card, you'll see individual bird feathers or the hairs on a human head! Painting in this detail needs a steady hand, 20/20 vision, a very fine brush – and lots of practice. Indians have been doing it for hundreds of years, with the first miniatures painted on palm leaves to illustrate religious texts.

This mini swing festival is painted in gouache, a type of watercolour.

Trendy Mehndi

Indians dress to dazzle – and it's not just about the clothes. Mehndi is the art of painting patterns with a dye called henna, directly onto the skin. Before Hindu weddings there's a whole mehndi ceremony, where families party while the bride gets decorated. Designs are intricate and last for several weeks. Sometimes the groom's initials are drawn in too – one reason not to fall out!

Mehndi is usually done on the hands and feet.

Pongy Paint?

Handmade paper, silk, walls, skin... Indian artists paint on all these things! Madhubani art was traditionally done by women on the walls of their mud huts, though now they work on paper and canvas too. Bamboo sticks are used to apply natural colours, such as white from rice powder, red from sandalwood, yellow from turmeric, and black from... wait for it... cow dung blended with soot!

Madhubani paintings are packed with geometric patterns.

29

More Information

Websites

http://www.roughguides.com/destinations/asia/india/
All you need to prepare for a trip to India.

http://www.bbc.co.uk/nature/places/indian_subcontinent
Packed with info about India's amazing wildlife.

http://india.gov.in/india-glance
The information pages of India's government.

http://www.tajmahal.org.uk/
Read all about the magnificent Taj Mahal.

http://www.bbc.co.uk/schools/primaryhistory/indus_valley/
Explore the Indus Valley civilisation – includes a fun game.

https://www.cia.gov/library/publications/the-world-factbook/geos/in.html
The CIA World Factbook India page, with up-to-date info and statistics.

Apps

Google Earth by Google, Inc Explore India (and the rest of the world) from the sky – for free!

India Travel Guide by Triposo A bundle of background info, city guides, maps and phrasebooks.

Got India by Olivaw Software A free talking phrasebook in Hindi and Telegu.

Crazy Rickshaw by Imagination Consulting Services A driving game against the clock!

Times of India by Times Internet Limited News, photos, cricket scores, movie reviews and more.

Movies

Gandhi, 1982 (PG)
A multi-award-winning epic following the life of Mahatma Gandhi, the peaceful revolutionary who helped India to gain independence.

3 Idiots, 2009 (12A)
The highest-grossing Bollywood film of all time – a comedy, starring Aamir Khan.

Wild India (National Geographic series)
Real-life drama in the Indian wilds, from forest tigers to desert lions.

Clips

http://www.bbc.co.uk/learningzone/clips/an-introduction-to-india/4602.html
A summary of India, its landscapes and climate.

http://www.youtube.com/watch?v=mmV_kWtkbPi
A dazzling song and dance routine from Bollywood.

http://video.nationalgeographic.co.uk/video/kids/people-places-kids/diwali-lights-festival-kids/
Check out Diwali, the Hindu festival of lights.

http://www.geobeats.com/video/1c4f45/dabbawalas
Meet Mumbai's tiffin-tastic dabbawalas.

http://kids.nationalgeographic.co.uk/kids/places/find/india/
Click on the Video tab to see the story of India's railways.

Books

20th Century Lives: Bollywood Stars by Liz Gogerly
(Wayland, 2010)

Countries Around the World: India by Ali Brownlie Bojang
(Raintree, 2013)

Developing World: India and Mumbai by Jenny Vaughan
(Franklin Watts, 2013)

Discover Countries: India by Tim Atkinson
(Wayland, 2012)

Journey Along a River: The Ganges by Paul Harrison
(Wayland, 2013)

Radar: Dance Culture: Bhangra and Bollywood by Anna Claybourne
(Wayland, 2011)

To wear a sari, the traditional Indian women's dress, you need a strip of fabric 5-8m long! A lungi is a shorter cloth that men wrap round their waist like a sarong.

Glossary

camouflaged – Blending in with the natural surroundings.

caste – A social class into which Hindus are born.

civilisation – An organised society with systems of government, culture, industry and so on.

endangered – Seriously at risk of extinction (dying out).

Mughals – The Islamic dynasty that ruled most of India from the early 1500s to the mid-1700s.

nomad – Someone with no fixed home who moves from place to place in search of food, water and grazing.

paddy field – An irrigated or flooded area of land where rice is grown.

pilgrim – Someone who travels to a place of worship.

polo – A game a bit like hockey, played on horseback with a long mallet.

rural – Relating to the countryside, rather than towns.

sitar – A large, long-necked stringed instrument, played by plucking.

slum – An overcrowded urban area with very poor standards of living.

tanning – Converting animal hides into leather by soaking them in chemicals.

tiffin – A light meal, usually eaten around midday.

Index

Unpacked

Australia
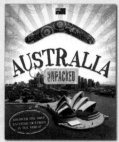

Australia: Unpacked
Exploration and Discovery
City Sights
Not All Desert
Aussie Animals
Long Distance Travellers
Go, Aussie, Go!
Mine Time
On the Coast
Native Australians
Aussie Tucker
Everyday Life
Coming to Australia

978 0 7502 7726 6

Brazil

Brazil: Unpacked
A World of Faces
Let's Go to Rio!
Viva Futebol!
Jungle Giant
Nature's Treasure Trove
Highways and Skyways
Bright Lights, Big Cities
Life, Brazilian Style
Looking Good
Arts for All
Adventurous Tastes
Prepare to Party!

978 0 7502 7997 0

France

France: Unpacked
The City of Light
Ruling France
Fruit of the Earth
Home and Away
Power and Progress
Grand Designs
Bon Appetit
The Arts
En Vacance
Made in France
Allez Sport
Life in France

978 0 7502 7728 0

India

India: Unpacked
From 0 to a Billion
Touring India
Everyone's Game
Wild Wonders
Rocks, Rivers, Rains
Life on the Land
High-tech, Low-tech!
Staggering Cities
Everyday India
Spice is Nice
Bollywood Beats
Bright Arts

978 0 7502 7725 9

Italy

Italy: Unpacked
The Romans
Rome: the Eternal City
Way to Go
Food Glorious Food
La Bella Figura
Mountains and Volcanoes
The Italian Arts
Calcio!
North and South
Everyday Life
Super Cities
Italian Inventions

978 0 7502 7727 3

Portugal

Portugal: Unpacked
Small Country, Big Story
Let's Play!
Holiday Hotspot
Sun, Sand and Serras
Island Magic
Charismatic Cities
Made in Portugal!
Country Corkers
Wild Times
Make Yourself at Home
Surf 'n Turf
Creative Culture

978 0 7502 7886 7

South Africa

South Africa: Unpacked
Three Capitals
The Land
Becoming South Africa
SA Sport
Farming
Rainbow Nation
Fabulous Food
Rich and Poor
Wild Life
Mineral Wealth
On the Coast
Holidays and Festivals

978 0 7502 7729 7

Spain

Spain: Unpacked
A World of Their Own
Fiesta Forever
On the Ball
Highlands and Islands
Sleepless Cities
Escape to the Country
Wild Spain
Spanish Life
All You Can Eat
Hola World!
Olé, Olé!
Eye-Popping Arts

978 0 7502 7730 3

WAYLAND
www.waylandbooks.co.uk